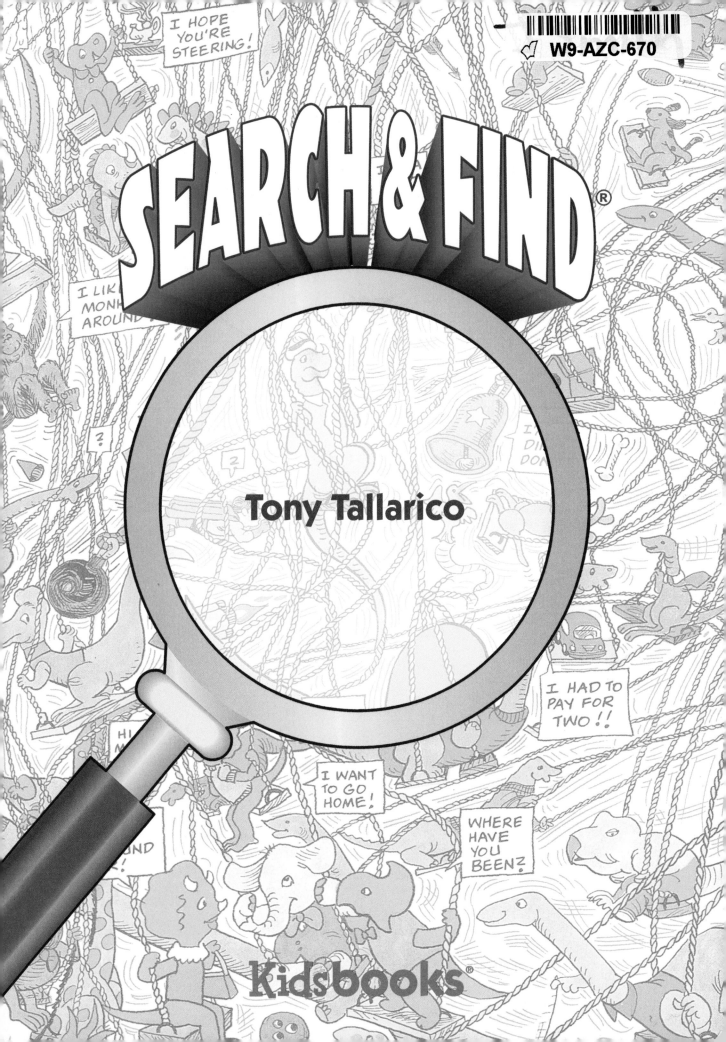

DETECT DONALD

Detect Donald at the **Cheez-E Diner** and...

Detect Donald
in the
Middle
Ages
and...

Detect Donald
in
Cartoonland
and...

- ☑ Baseball bats (2)
- ☐ Bees (4)
- ☐ Broom
- ☐ Burst balloon
- ☐ Cats (5)
- ☐ Chicken
- ☐ Crow
- ☐ Elephants (2)
- ☐ Elf
- ☐ Firefighter
- ☐ Gingerbread man
- ☐ Golf tee
- ☐ Horses (2)
- ☐ Hot dog
- ☐ Lamp
- ☐ Masks (2)
- ☐ Mushroom
- ☐ Pie
- ☐ Pirate hat
- ☐ Pot
- ☐ Rabbit
- ☐ Saxophone
- ☐ Scarf
- ☐ Snake
- ☐ Swiss cheese
- ☐ Underwear

Detect Donald
at the
Pirates' Battle
and...

Detect Donald
in the
Future
and...

- ☐ Apple
- ☐ Cactus
- ☐ Christmas ornament
- ☐ Clock
- ☐ Curly thing
- ☐ Ear
- ☐ Elephant
- ☐ Evergreen tree
- ☐ Fish
- ☐ Football
- ☐ Football helmet
- ☐ Fork
- ☐ Graduate's hat
- ☐ Guitar
- ☐ Ice-cream cone
- ☐ Ice skate
- ☐ Jester
- ☐ Nail
- ☐ Owl
- ☐ Paintbrush
- ☐ Postage stamp
- ☐ Roller skate
- ☐ Santa Claus
- ☐ Skateboard
- ☐ Spoon
- ☐ Stop sign

Detect Donald in
Napoleon's France
and...

- ☐ Alien
- ☐ Arrow
- ☐ Basket
- ☐ Basketball players (2)
- ☐ Baton twirler
- ☐ Bear
- ☐ Bowling ball
- ☐ Cardboard box
- ☐ Crown
- ☐ Fishing pole
- ☐ French bread
- ☐ Garbage can
- ☐ Haystack
- ☐ Ice-cream cone
- ☐ Jack-o'-lantern
- ☐ Key
- ☐ Lost boot
- ☐ Mask
- ☐ Mouse
- ☐ Net
- ☐ Paintbrush
- ☐ Propeller
- ☐ Red bird
- ☐ Rooster
- ☐ Skull
- ☐ Tin can
- ☐ Turtle

Detect Donald
at
Fort Knocks
and...

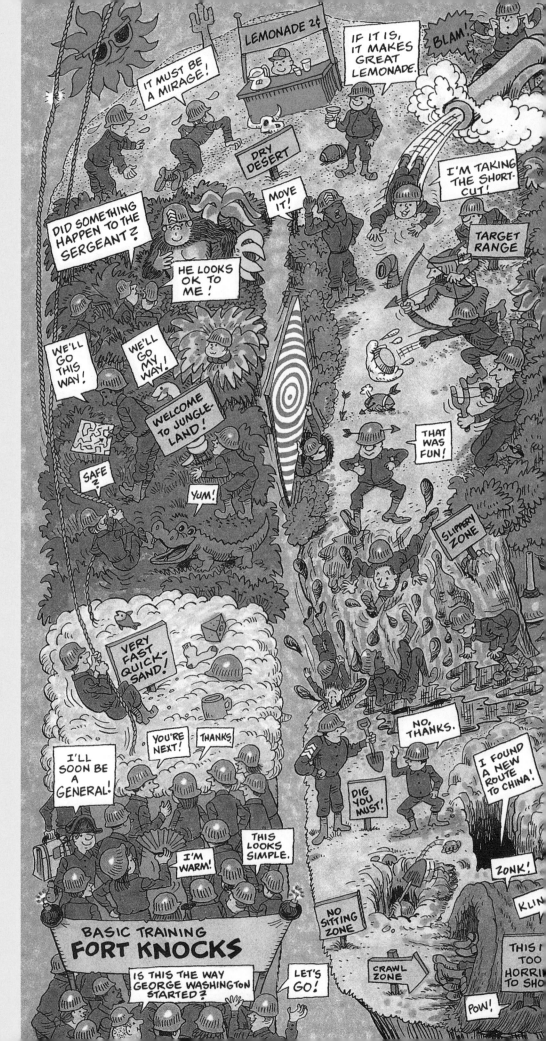

Detect Donald
in
Ancient Rome
and...

- ☐ Arrow
- ☐ Backwards helmet
- ☐ Balloon
- ☐ Cactus
- ☐ Cat
- ☐ Emperor
- ☐ Falling rock
- ☐ Flower
- ☐ Horseless chariot
- ☐ Jack-o'-lantern
- ☐ Julius and Augustus
- ☐ Mask
- ☐ Movie director
- ☐ Painted egg
- ☐ Pig
- ☐ Pizza box
- ☐ Puddles (2)
- ☐ Rabbit
- ☐ Shield
- ☐ Skull
- ☐ Slice of pizza
- ☐ Snake
- ☐ Sock
- ☐ Spears (2)
- ☐ Star
- ☐ Tire

Detect Donald in
Prehistoric Times
and...

Detect **Donald** at the **Academy Awards** and...

LOOK FOR LAURA DETECT DONALD FIND FRANKIE SEARCH FOR SUSIE

FIND FRANKIE

Find Frankie at the Monster Club Meeting and...

- ☐ Bow ties (3)
- ☐ Bug
- ☐ Cane
- ☐ Cracked mirror
- ☐ Elephant
- ☐ Eyeglasses
- ☐ Insect
- ☐ Knight in armor
- ☐ Mouse holes (2)
- ☐ Mummy
- ☐ Neckties (4)
- ☐ Parrot
- ☐ Pirate
- ☐ Propeller
- ☐ Rain boots
- ☐ Scar
- ☐ Shelves (2)
- ☐ Ski hat
- ☐ Smelly monster
- ☐ Snake
- ☐ Straw
- ☐ Suspenders
- ☐ Towel
- ☐ Turtle
- ☐ Witch
- ☐ Wooden club

Find Frankie
on the
Street
and...

- ☐ Benches (2)
- ☐ Books (2)
- ☐ Candle
- ☐ Clowns (2)
- ☐ Crayon
- ☐ Crowns (2)
- ☐ Dogs (2)
- ☐ Dripping faucet
- ☐ Duck
- ☐ Fish
- ☐ Flowerpots (2)
- ☐ Handbag
- ☐ Hard hat
- ☐ Jogger
- ☐ Man sleeping
- ☐ Mouse ears
- ☐ Newspaper
- ☐ Parrot
- ☐ Peanut
- ☐ Pinocchio
- ☐ Postal worker
- ☐ Sailor hats (2)
- ☐ Sombrero
- ☐ Spaceman
- ☐ Suspenders (3 sets)
- ☐ Tepee
- ☐ Toolbox
- ☐ Umbrella

Find Frankie in the Supermarket and...

- ☑ Bandanas (3)
- ☑ Bare foot
- ☐ Broom
- ☐ Cobweb
- ☐ Cook
- ☐ Cowboy
- ☐ Crown
- ☐ Dog fish
- ☐ Eggs
- ☐ Firefighter
- ☐ Fire hydrant
- ☐ Fishing pole
- ☐ Football player
- ☐ Handbag
- ☐ Jack-in-the-box
- ☐ Knee pads
- ☐ Paddles (2)
- ☐ Pear
- ☐ People sleeping (2)
- ☐ Pocket watch
- ☐ Pole-vaulter
- ☐ Propeller
- ☐ Scarves (2)
- ☐ Snake
- ☐ Straw
- ☐ Sunglasses
- ☐ Swordfish
- ☐ Toaster

Find Frankie at the
Theater
and...

- ☐ Ballerina
- ☐ Bare feet (3)
- ☐ Baseball cap
- ☐ Beard
- ☐ Boat
- ☐ Candy cane
- ☐ Cane
- ☐ Cannon
- ☐ Cigar
- ☐ Cowboys (2)
- ☐ Flying shoe
- ☐ Gorilla
- ☐ Graduate's hat
- ☐ Helmet with horns (2)
- ☐ High-top sneaker
- ☐ Hot dog
- ☐ Ladders (2)
- ☐ Man in the moon
- ☐ Owl
- ☐ Paper airplane
- ☐ Propeller
- ☐ Scar
- ☐ Sheep
- ☐ Skull
- ☐ Suspenders (2 pairs)
- ☐ Target
- ☐ Tent

Find Frankie at the **Zoo** and...

- ☐ Alligator
- ☐ Artist
- ☐ Blue hats (3)
- ☐ Bucket
- ☐ Carrots (2)
- ☐ Clothesline
- ☐ Fishing pole
- ☐ Half-moon
- ☐ Jack-o'-lantern
- ☐ Kids on father's shoulder (2)
- ☐ Knee pads
- ☐ Ladder
- ☐ Matador
- ☐ Monkey
- ☐ Orange birds (2)
- ☐ Park bench
- ☐ Periscope
- ☐ Pink flamingo
- ☐ Purple hats (3)
- ☐ Rabbits (2)
- ☐ Red bandanas (2)
- ☐ Red hats (4)
- ☐ Stool
- ☐ Strollers (2)
- ☐ Tiger
- ☐ Umbrella
- ☐ Zookeepers (3)

Find Frankie at the Yum-Yum Emporium and...

- ☐ Alien
- ☐ Baseball cap
- ☐ Bib
- ☐ Book
- ☐ Booster seat
- ☐ Briefcase
- ☐ Crown
- ☐ Crutch
- ☐ Cupcake
- ☐ Duck
- ☐ Eyeglasses (7)
- ☐ Eye patch
- ☐ Food fight
- ☐ Football player
- ☐ Ice-cream cone
- ☐ Mailbox
- ☐ Man with fingers in ears
- ☐ Napkin dispensers (2)
- ☐ Pearl necklaces (2)
- ☐ Pig
- ☐ Pizza
- ☐ Rain slicker
- ☐ Red bandanas (2)
- ☐ Red hats (2)
- ☐ Salt shaker
- ☐ Shark fin

Find Frankie at the Aquarium and...

- ☐ Backpack
- ☐ Bottle
- ☐ Camera
- ☐ Cowboy
- ☐ Doghouses (2)
- ☐ Electric eel
- ☐ Faucet
- ☐ Ghost
- ☐ Green handbag
- ☐ Lamp
- ☐ Mushroom
- ☐ Net
- ☐ Robot
- ☐ Rocking horse
- ☐ Rowboat
- ☐ Sailboat
- ☐ Sailor hat
- ☐ Scooter
- ☐ Sharks (2)
- ☐ Snorkel & mask
- ☐ Snowman
- ☐ Snowshoes
- ☐ Starfish (3)
- ☐ Swords (2)
- ☐ Teacher
- ☐ Telescope
- ☐ Tin man
- ☐ Turtles (3)

Find Frankie at the Rowdy Roller Rink and...

- ☐ Arrow
- ☐ Baby
- ☐ Balloons (3)
- ☐ Bird
- ☐ Buffalo
- ☐ Cactus
- ☐ Candle
- ☐ Clowns (2)
- ☐ Deer
- ☐ Dinosaur
- ☐ Dogs (3)
- ☐ Fairy godmother
- ☐ Hamburger
- ☐ Heart
- ☐ Jester hat
- ☐ Jump rope
- ☐ Knight
- ☐ Lamp shade
- ☐ Manhole
- ☐ Mouse
- ☐ Paintbrushes (2)
- ☐ "Pigman"
- ☐ Pizza
- ☐ Sheep
- ☐ Sombrero
- ☐ Suspenders
- ☐ Tennis racquet

Find Frankie in the **Arcade** and...

- ☐ Balloon
- ☐ Beach ball
- ☐ Bees (2)
- ☐ Birdcage
- ☐ Black cat
- ☐ Book
- ☐ Bucket
- ☐ Cannon
- ☐ Dracula
- ☐ Faucet
- ☐ Football
- ☐ Hard hat
- ☐ Jack-o'-lantern
- ☐ Lightning
- ☐ Maze
- ☐ Mouse
- ☐ Mummy
- ☐ Policeman
- ☐ Rocket
- ☐ Sailor hat
- ☐ Stuffed animal
- ☐ Suitcase
- ☐ Sunglasses
- ☐ Target
- ☐ Top hat
- ☐ Turtle
- ☐ Umbrella
- ☐ Yo-yo

Find Frankie in the **Suburbs** and...

- [ ] Basketball
- [ ] Bat
- [ ] Bone
- [ ] Books (3)
- [ ] Broken window
- [ ] Broom
- [ ] "Dead End"
- [ ] Gate
- [ ] Ghost
- [ ] Golf bag
- [ ] Guitar
- [ ] Hammock
- [ ] Haunted house
- [ ] Jogger
- [ ] Jump rope
- [ ] Mailbox
- [ ] Mail delivery
- [ ] Monster hands (2)
- [ ] Mouse
- [ ] Rabbit
- [ ] Shovel
- [ ] Snake
- [ ] Sunglasses
- [ ] Superhero
- [ ] Tea bag
- [ ] Tire swing
- [ ] Trash cans (3)
- [ ] Tuba

Find Frankie at the Monsters' New Clubhouse and...

- ☐ Backpack
- ☐ Bee
- ☐ Broom
- ☐ Candles (2)
- ☐ Clouds (2)
- ☐ Cobweb
- ☐ Doormat
- ☐ Eyeglasses
- ☐ Flower
- ☐ Heart
- ☐ Mouse hole
- ☐ Mustache
- ☐ Neckties (2)
- ☐ Octopus
- ☐ Pencil
- ☐ Pirate
- ☐ Pointed hats (2)
- ☐ Smiling ghosts (2)
- ☐ Smiling star
- ☐ Snake
- ☐ Thirteens (4)
- ☐ Tic-tac-toe
- ☐ Tiny monster
- ☐ Trapdoor
- ☐ Trees (2)
- ☐ Turtle
- ☐ Umbrella
- ☐ Unhappy moon

FIND FRANKIE   SEARCH FOR SUSIE   LOOK FOR LAURA   DETECT DONALD

LOOK FOR LAURA

Look for Laura on the Planet Maxxx and...

- ☐ Asteroid for rent
- ☐ Banana
- ☐ Baseball
- ☐ Birds (2)
- ☐ Briefcase
- ☐ Broom
- ☐ Clocks (4)
- ☐ Duck
- ☐ Fork
- ☐ Hammer
- ☐ Helmet
- ☐ Horse
- ☐ Hot dog
- ☐ Monkey
- ☐ Moon
- ☐ Mushroom
- ☐ Paper airplane
- ☐ Plumber's plunger
- ☐ Pyramid
- ☐ Robot
- ☐ Skateboard
- ☐ Snake
- ☐ Star
- ☐ Sunglasses
- ☐ Tire
- ☐ Tree

Look for Laura in the Ocean and...

- ☐ Baseball bat
- ☐ Birdhouse
- ☐ Bottle
- ☐ Cheese
- ☐ Crown
- ☐ Duck
- ☐ Empty turtle shell
- ☐ Fishhook
- ☐ Flowerpot
- ☐ Football
- ☐ Fork
- ☐ Graduate's hat
- ☐ Key
- ☐ Life preserver
- ☐ Lollipop
- ☐ Milk carton
- ☐ Net
- ☐ Old boot
- ☐ Pear
- ☐ Pointed hat
- ☐ Pot
- ☐ Sailboat
- ☐ Screwdriver
- ☐ Sea horse
- ☐ Snorkel & mask
- ☐ Starfish
- ☐ Sword

Look for Laura at the
Watering Hole
and...

- ☐ Baby bird
- ☐ Birdcage
- ☐ Briefcase
- ☐ Chickens (2)
- ☐ Clothespins (2)
- ☐ Coconuts (4)
- ☐ Donkey
- ☐ Duck
- ☐ Feather
- ☐ Fish (3)
- ☐ Headband
- ☐ Heart
- ☐ Hippo
- ☐ Leopard
- ☐ Lions (2)
- ☐ Log
- ☐ Octopus
- ☐ Ping-Pong paddle
- ☐ Radio
- ☐ Rhinoceros
- ☐ Robot
- ☐ Turtle
- ☐ TV set
- ☐ Worm

Look for Laura
on a
Ski Slope
in the **Alps**
and...

- [ ] Balloon
- [ ] Barrels (2)
- [ ] Car
- [ ] Duck
- [ ] Earmuffs (3 pairs)
- [ ] Easel
- [ ] Elephant
- [ ] Frankenstein's monster
- [ ] Glove
- [ ] Headbands (2)
- [ ] Lamppost
- [ ] Lost boots (2)
- [ ] Lost ski
- [ ] Red bows (3)
- [ ] Scarves (7)
- [ ] Scuba diver
- [ ] Shovel
- [ ] "Soft Snow"
- [ ] Sunbather
- [ ] Telephone
- [ ] Telescope
- [ ] Tent
- [ ] Thrown snowball
- [ ] Train
- [ ] Tree

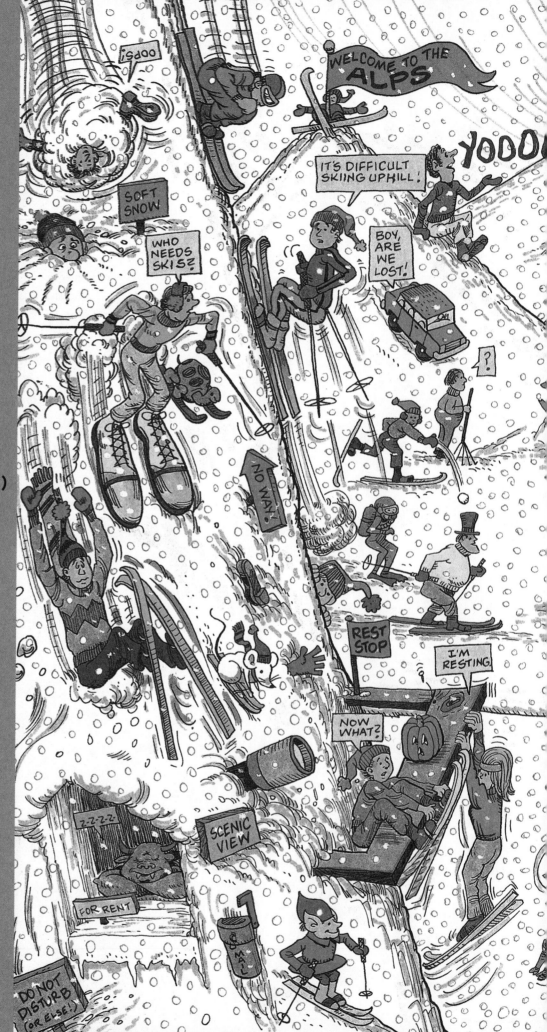

Look for Laura in
Europe
and...

Look for **Laura** at

Summer Camp

and...

Look for **Laura** at the **Circus** and...

- [ ] Bandanas (2)
- [ ] Bicycle
- [ ] Bird
- [ ] Broom
- [ ] Car
- [ ] Cat
- [ ] Crown
- [ ] Drum
- [ ] Earmuff
- [ ] Flowerpot
- [ ] Flying shoe
- [ ] Football helmet
- [ ] Giraffe
- [ ] Lamp
- [ ] Mustaches (4)
- [ ] Padlock
- [ ] Paper bag
- [ ] Periscope
- [ ] Pointed hats (3)
- [ ] Propeller
- [ ] Rabbit
- [ ] Ring of fire
- [ ] Sailor
- [ ] Santa Claus
- [ ] Straw hat
- [ ] Unhappy face
- [ ] Unicorn
- [ ] Whip

Look for **Laura** in **Washington DC** and...

- ☐ Baby kangaroo
- ☐ Balloons (2)
- ☐ Baseball cap
- ☐ Basket
- ☐ Capitol Building
- ☐ Dog
- ☐ Duck
- ☐ FBI agent
- ☐ Gloves
- ☐ Headband
- ☐ Jefferson Memorial
- ☐ Kite
- ☐ Mailbox
- ☐ Manhole
- ☐ Mouse
- ☐ Neckties (2)
- ☐ Paintbrush
- ☐ Pillow
- ☐ Ponytails (3)
- ☐ Red beret
- ☐ Red socks (4 pairs)
- ☐ Rope
- ☐ Sailor hat
- ☐ Spirit of St. Louis
- ☐ Sunglasses
- ☐ Tri-cornered hat
- ☐ Upside-down sign
- ☐ Wagon

Look for **Laura** at **School** and...

- ☐ Basketball
- ☐ Birdhouse
- ☐ Bookend
- ☐ Boot
- ☐ Clock
- ☐ Cupcake
- ☐ Dog
- ☐ Drum set
- ☐ Earmuffs
- ☐ Eyeglasses (3)
- ☐ Fork
- ☐ Globe
- ☐ Hair bows (5)
- ☐ Joke book
- ☐ Jump rope
- ☐ Mitten
- ☐ Nail
- ☐ Pen
- ☐ Pencils (4)
- ☐ Rabbit
- ☐ Scarf
- ☐ Soccer ball
- ☐ Sock
- ☐ Straw hat
- ☐ Teddy bear
- ☐ Three-legged stool
- ☐ Tic-tac-toe
- ☐ Top hat

Look for **Laura** at the
Welcome
Home Party
and...

- ☐ Balloons (2)
- ☐ Baseball
- ☐ Boot
- ☐ Bouquet of flowers
- ☐ Bowling ball
- ☐ Broom
- ☐ Dog
- ☐ Donut
- ☐ Fish
- ☐ Flowerpot
- ☐ Half-moons (2)
- ☐ Hearts (2)
- ☐ Ice-cream cone
- ☐ Manhole
- ☐ Nose
- ☐ Old tire
- ☐ Paddle
- ☐ Pail
- ☐ Pocket watch
- ☐ Scissors
- ☐ Screwdriver
- ☐ Stars (8)
- ☐ Straw
- ☐ Sunglasses
- ☐ Swiss cheese
- ☐ Top hat
- ☐ Turtle

DETECT DONALD   FIND FRANKIE   SEARCH FOR SUSIE   LOOK FOR LAURA

SEARCH FOR SUSIE

Search for Susie at the Water Ride and...

- ☐ Apple
- ☐ Beach ball
- ☐ Bib
- ☐ Bull
- ☐ Candles (2)
- ☐ Cats (2)
- ☐ Earring
- ☐ Elephants (2)
- ☐ Fishing pole
- ☐ Gorilla
- ☐ Hearts (2)
- ☐ Hot dog
- ☐ Kangaroo
- ☐ Paper bag
- ☐ Parrot
- ☐ Pencil
- ☐ Periscope
- ☐ Picnic basket
- ☐ Pitcher
- ☐ Puddles (4)
- ☐ Rabbits (2)
- ☐ Scuba diver
- ☐ Sheep
- ☐ Snakes (2)
- ☐ Sunglasses (2)
- ☐ Tents (3)
- ☐ Tire

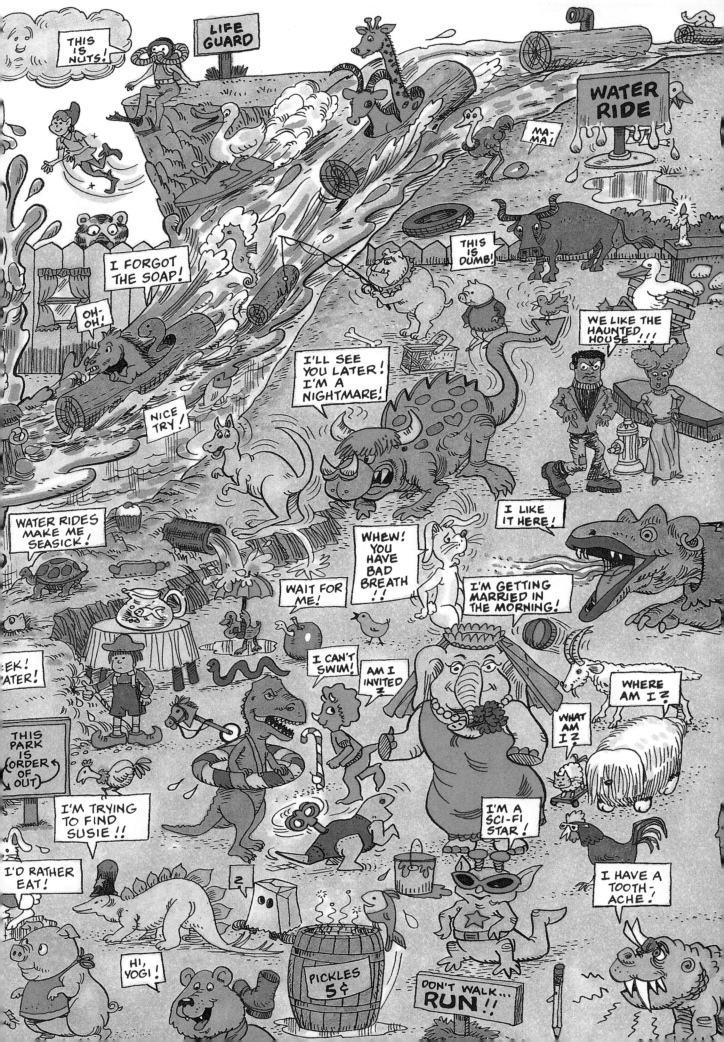

Search for Susie at the Carousel and...

Search for Susie at the **Fun House** and...

- ☐ Airplane
- ☐ Alligator
- ☐ Anchor
- ☐ Arrows (2)
- ☐ Baseball cap
- ☐ Book
- ☐ Bowling ball
- ☐ Cactus
- ☐ Candle
- ☐ Chef's hat
- ☐ Clothespin
- ☐ Curtains
- ☐ Diving board
- ☐ Fish
- ☐ Flowers (2)
- ☐ Football
- ☐ Giraffes (2)
- ☐ Lamp
- ☐ Lollipop
- ☐ Lost boots (2)
- ☐ Masks (2)
- ☐ Mice (2)
- ☐ Pinocchio
- ☐ Rabbits (3)
- ☐ Sailor hat
- ☐ Turtles (2)
- ☐ TV set
- ☐ Vase

Search for Susie at the Ferris Wheel and...

- ☐ Alarm clock
- ☐ Barrel
- ☐ Broken eggs
- ☐ Coffeepot
- ☐ Dog
- ☐ Ducks (3)
- ☐ Elephant
- ☐ Flowers (2)
- ☐ Football
- ☐ Giraffe
- ☐ Gorilla
- ☐ Guitar
- ☐ Happy face
- ☐ Helicopter
- ☐ Jack-o'-lantern
- ☐ Jeep
- ☐ Ladders (2)
- ☐ Lions (2)
- ☐ Lost sneaker
- ☐ Mice (2)
- ☐ Neckties (4)
- ☐ Owl
- ☐ Paintbrushes (2)
- ☐ Quicksand
- ☐ Red flowers (2)
- ☐ Shovel
- ☐ Snake

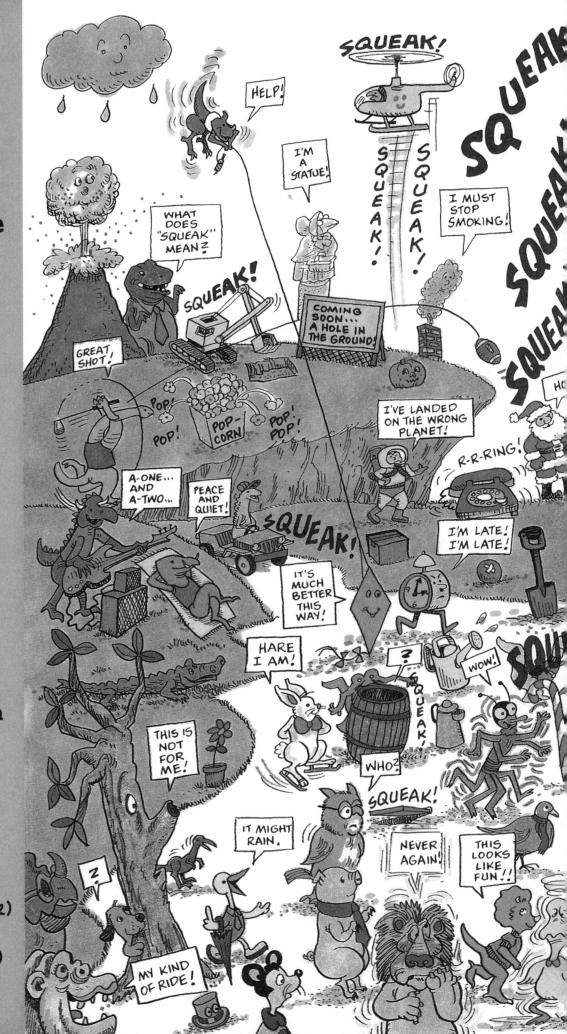

Search for Susie on the Rock and Roller Coaster and...

- ☐ Barbell
- ☐ Beach ball
- ☐ Bowling ball
- ☐ Buffalo
- ☐ Cactus
- ☐ Candy cane
- ☐ Doghouse
- ☐ Dogs (2)
- ☐ Dollar sign
- ☐ Eight ball
- ☐ Elephants (2)
- ☐ Fishercat
- ☐ Football
- ☐ Giraffes (3)
- ☐ Hockey stick
- ☐ Hot dog
- ☐ Ice-cream cone
- ☐ Mice (3)
- ☐ Pencil
- ☐ Periscope
- ☐ Pigs (2)
- ☐ Pot
- ☐ Snake
- ☐ Swings
- ☐ Target
- ☐ Telescope
- ☐ Tin can
- ☐ Train engine

Search for Susie in the Game Room and...

- ☐ Banana
- ☐ Blindfold
- ☐ Bucket
- ☐ Cat
- ☐ Catcher's mitt
- ☐ Donkeys (2)
- ☐ "Don't Be Quiet"
- ☐ Dustpan
- ☐ Fake nose
- ☐ Flying reptile
- ☐ Football
- ☐ Graduate's hat
- ☐ Green bug
- ☐ Guitar
- ☐ Hairbrush
- ☐ Juggler
- ☐ Kangaroo
- ☐ Magnifying glass
- ☐ Mouse house
- ☐ Picture frame
- ☐ Pie
- ☐ Rabbits (3)
- ☐ Ring toss
- ☐ Roller skate
- ☐ Scarf
- ☐ Snake
- ☐ Toolbox

Search for Susie on the Bumper Cars and...

- [ ] Alligator
- [ ] Automobile
- [ ] Banana peel
- [ ] Baseball cap
- [ ] Birds (3)
- [ ] Bow ties (2)
- [ ] Easel
- [ ] Elephants (2)
- [ ] Football player
- [ ] Lions (2)
- [ ] Manhole
- [ ] Necklace
- [ ] Old shoe
- [ ] Paintbrush
- [ ] "Pay Toll Here"
- [ ] Propeller
- [ ] Rope
- [ ] Sailboat
- [ ] Scarves (2)
- [ ] Seal
- [ ] Snake
- [ ] Sneaker car
- [ ] Straw
- [ ] Surfboard
- [ ] Table
- [ ] Tiger
- [ ] Top hat

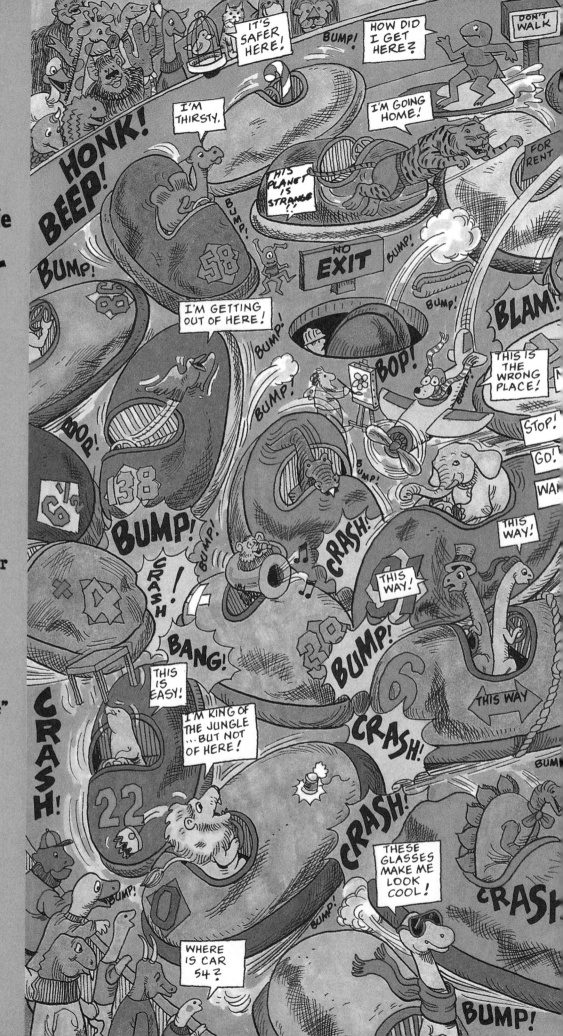

Search for Susie at the Ice Cream Shop and...

- ☐ Alien
- ☐ Banana peel
- ☐ Bowling ball
- ☐ Bubble gum
- ☐ Cactus
- ☐ Camel
- ☐ Candy cane
- ☐ Can of paint
- ☐ Clown
- ☐ Cow
- ☐ Flowerpot
- ☐ Flying carpet
- ☐ Flying reptiles (2)
- ☐ Football helmet
- ☐ Mice (3)
- ☐ Nail
- ☐ Parrot
- ☐ Pig
- ☐ Pillow
- ☐ Pocket watch
- ☐ Propeller hat
- ☐ Rocking horse
- ☐ Sailor hat
- ☐ Shovel
- ☐ Snake
- ☐ Star
- ☐ Straw

Search for Susie on the Giant Swings and...

- ☐ Arrow
- ☐ Baseball caps (2)
- ☐ Bears (2)
- ☐ Birdcage
- ☐ Bowling ball
- ☐ Broom
- ☐ Cat
- ☐ Dart
- ☐ Dogs (2)
- ☐ Elephants (2)
- ☐ Fishhook
- ☐ Football helmet
- ☐ Hot dog
- ☐ Lamps (2)
- ☐ Lollipop
- ☐ Lost sneaker
- ☐ Magic lamp
- ☐ Monkey
- ☐ Mouse
- ☐ Penguin
- ☐ Propeller
- ☐ Rocket
- ☐ Snake
- ☐ Soccer ball
- ☐ Sock
- ☐ Superhero
- ☐ Yo-yo